LIVING INSPIRED

Loretta Moore

ISBN: 978-81-19228-80-5

First Edition: 2023
Rs. 200/-

Cyberwit.net
HIG 45 Kaushambi Kunj, Kalindipuram
Allahabad - 211011 (U.P.) India
http://www.cyberwit.net
Tel: +(91) 9415091004
E-mail: info@cyberwit.net

The Lord is my Refuge, a Presence and Place of Peace. I am living inspired.

Contents

UNDER HIS WINGS

Humanity appears to be sinking into hedonism; it seems mankind has departed from the Will of God. Society needs to cease celebrating unrighteous living, take back life this wrongful world has stolen, for the 'marvelous' experience Christ Jesus has for you 'Under His Wings'.

The shattering truth, based on this 'demented generation', it seems mankind has adopted a senseless, purposeless, misdirected way of life, and is unwilling to conduct life according to the way, the truth and the life as put forth by God.

The Lord beckons on His Holy ground to wrest you from this wretched world, He can reward you with a better, righteous experience. Let the Savior's Light shine on your life. Glorify the Lord for the battle you've won, for the peace, comfort, and love you've attained 'Under His Wings'.

The Lord God Is a Cure-All

We tend to feel helpless in these worldly times—it can seem as if we're sinking into a darkened, hopeless never-neverland. It appears we have stopped pursuing a good, wholesome, value-structured lifestyle and allowed damning, degrading measures to overwhelm society. We find ourselves struggling in a disoriented, blame-worthy culture. A dismal, stagnant, unrewarding world has overtaken society, but there is hope for an upturn in every circumstance, a totally life transformation because the Lord God is a Cure-All.

TOO MUCH IS GOING WRONG

A moral compass has been rejected, and a sense of decency forfeited. Society finds itself operating in a reckless, vile, indecent, worldly, self-glorifying lifestyle.

There's no calm world-wide with the uptick of animus, radicalism and violence. The world is rife with eruption, and disrupting elements. Where has adherence to goodness gone? Social incompatibility has pushed society into social unrest. Could we be wading in moral decay? An opposing force seems to have transformed and desensitized our human capacity, sensibilities, and sense of decency, replacing it with self-absorption, self-aggrandizement and incivility. For certain, there's too much going wrong.

When my thoughts turn to what's going on with young people in American society I see a decline in standards, a media component has aided. It seems a renegade spirit has taken over. Too much is going wrong.

CHRISTIAN ARMOR

As much as we human beings want to feel in control, we must keep a watchful eye on daily thoughts and deeds, for a fall in character is just waiting to happen.

The struggle is constant, and we can never surrender to feelings that tempt because one instance of indiscretion can discredit us forever.

My advice...put on your Christian armor, and ascribe to righteousness.

With so many things to corrupt our values, we need the heavy protection of a Christian life to be guarded from the evils of the world. A relationship with Christ Jesus allows us to travel through this wretched land unafraid of being assailed.

Be careful not to hand over the control to those who would color your life with darkness and failure. (As a faithful observer of society I feel compelled to make this revelation: There can be strangers or relatives who wish you 'ill-will', and this even as they appear to have the best intentions. Their aim is to make you utterly miserable and unhappy.)

Nonetheless, if you have put the control in the Lord's hand you are wearing your Christian armor, and no weapon formed against you can prosper.

This World Is a Decadent Betrayer.

If you're feeling lost, unsteady, maladjusted, bewildered, joyless, you're probably living according to life's unwieldy command, demands, and suffering because this world is a decadent betrayer.

If you're seeking a way out of this whirling dark habitation know that human frailty cannot match the world's adversarial domination and demands. However God is an enriching, remarkable covering, a light for the darkness, an unmovable shelter— in His Hands you have peace surpassing all understanding. The Lord has everything you lack, everything to make your life whole and protected because this world is a decadent betrayer.

THIS TROUBLED WORLD!!!

The world and what it 'advocates' has taken society beyond the bounds God intended, period!

We've allowed many things to interrupt, and set the course for our lives. The influences are many depositing a confounding, unrighteous, immoral spirit into society at large. A worldly, pleasurable, magical mixture through entertainment, the media and other outward operating sources are overwhelmingly communicating what is 'Abominable' in the sight of the Lord—promoting the 'Sinful' nature in mankind. A worldly experience and all that it embraces represents Nothing good, and in truth living according this immoral, pleasure-seeking world falsifies life. Be aware that it presents the worst, and what is 'Damnation' at work; it's unable to fulfill, offers 'Void', brings into life disaster, trouble, suffering and a bitter end.

In this troubled world in which we live, although the trail might feel lonesome without pursuing 'superficial pleasures' worldliness represents, life seems void and empty because you haven't handed your life over to God for the Way, the Truth, and the Life!

Blacks and Progress

The opportunity to fully embrace the promise America purports hasn't happened. Others have been through only a fraction of the adversity Blacks have experienced. As such it's no mystery that they've lagged behind achieving advances and opportunities that were shaded by guile, or just plainly withheld. Nonetheless, great progress has been made, and the light of hope still shines for further Black advancement.

No Longer Safe In America

Feeling safe and secure is no longer the case in America!

Americans have had to witness the 'comfortable life' that was normal become eroded by violence and crime, and other things contrary and averse to what used to substantiate society.

To a great degree, 'drugs' and 'guns' are responsible for the revved up criminal behavior destroying the sensible, sound American experience that once was.

I mentioned 'drugs' and 'guns' as the culprits devastating America, a culture that embraces safety, security, and prosperity, however, other factors can be contributors. Looking at environment, specifically at 'households', deficient nurturing, fatherlessness, economic insufficiency, violent, criminal surroundings, and numerous other degrading factors defy a basis for normal physical and mental development.

Circumstances help form mental abnormalities and human malfunction that lead to compulsive, self-destructive, deleterious behavior, thus, 'drugs' and 'guns' and other destructive involvement.

We need to pray that the Lord will show the way back to the safe, secure America we used to enjoy.

"America Needed to Deescalate and Decompress"

In the 'midst' of this horrific Strange-land experience, society has become more cognizant, more aware of meaningful, simplistic things of life. We now live in a 'mist' of confusion, having been drastically downsized from a manufactured aspirational, pleasure-seeking, high- hopes structured society.

We're at a bare-bones level, separated from an extravagant, extreme prior basis for living, though I think that we've come to learn just how 'spiritually' bereft we are.

YOU ARE GOD'S SEED-2

Break from this world's hard Captivity....
Remove yourself from suffering and depravity....
Step away from life's hard passages....
Come away from worldly ravages....
Stop being led by the devil, like a fool....
Be lifted from the world's dark, angry pool....
Let yourself go into the loving Hand of the Lord....
Be saved by His Will, Way and Holy Word....

God is what you need...You are God's seed....
God is what you need...You are God's seed...
God is what you need...You are God's seed.

LIFE HAS LOST ITS LUSTER

Today's life experience is embedded with disturbance, complication, abnormality and disaffection—unwelcomed transformation!

A solid comfortable shield once in place for living has been fractured, and America and the world have been confined to a strange, unwelcoming planet.

Exuberance, ambition, success, attainment, and love/romance no longer comfortably under-pin society. It's a new 'unrewarding' time since life has lost its luster.

Americans Have Let Down the Guardrails

Something disruptive and adversarial has changed American society. A highly contributing factor for the transformation seems to be a lack of control over personal conduct in the public arena. It seems to me parental guidance is at the core of the enormous societal problem! The loss of self-control seems attributable to the role the family used to play, now dismantled. And of course, economic disparity, and other contributing factors are actively reducing the solid American way of life.

Life seems to be pulling everyone apart into disparate pieces. As a society Americans have let down the guardrails of decency on everything imaginable!

Hollywood and the media had a transforming adverse effect globally. Movies and television, and more recently social media have sent glaring, defiling messages and images to society; entertainment has changed the course from a normally acceptable moral-based public to one that persuaded through indecency and perversion.

America has never veered from its intention to be an assimilated society, equalized organism, a naturally good-intentioned community. However, socially it is indiscernible from its original good intent, and has plummeted to a violent, vile, indecent low.

HIS SPIRITUAL PEACE

In this ungodly world, life is the antithesis of what society presumed it to be. In reality, we're vulnerable, discombobulated, and alarmed. We stand alone and fearful of what's around the bend, what's coming down the pike. We're a society, disarmed, helpless in the midst of a disturbed, counter-balanced experience. For certain, the things destabilizing and horrific in society will not cease. We're unable to assume the softer textures of life, the fullest essence for living that comes from God only and His spiritual peace.

In the 'midst' of this horrific Strange-land experience, society has become more cognizant, more aware of meaningful, simplistic things taken away from life. We now live in a 'mist' of confusion, having been drastically down-sized from a manufactured aspirational, pleasure-seeking, high- hopes structured society. (We're at a bare-bones level, separated from an extravagant, extreme prior basis for living, although I think that we've come to learn just how 'spiritually' bereft we are).

Happiness is only a presumption, and can never be fulfilled without the substantiation of the Lord God -we're lost pilgrims plodding along in a darkened world seeking the light of day. We're weak, unable to overcome the instability and turbulence and pressure the world has structured around us. Society world-wide needs a spiritual 'healing'.

The Lord alone can fortify, strengthen and solidify mankind with His spiritual Peace.

IN GOD'S HANDS

Society is experiencing a spiritual low. Everywhere havoc, danger, insanity, misery, and other kinds of hard-driving matters have settled around our lives.

Nevertheless, life can be so different, and lighter, better if we place ourselves and souls, "In God's Hands".

"We Are God's Gift"

The earth, the universe, everything belongs to God.

Looking around, I can't but marvel at the Gift God has presented us.

However, I have to say that He, the Lord made us as a part of that Gift. We are God's Gift.

The conditions of life can be devastating, pressing our spirits low. Nevertheless, the simplest things are signatures of a more joyous life; naturally, life holds incalculable displays of unexpected joy: a baby's smile, the woods across the way, a vase of lovely flowers, oceans, rivers, streams, countrysides, shorelines, paintings on a wall, and many other fleeting instances and glances that trigger a sense of well-being and even joy!

So whenever you're felling empty, unwanted, undesirable, concerned, unloved, it can be ever so 'reassuring' to remind yourself that we are God's Gift!

THIS HIGHLY DISFUNCTIONAL WORLD

Today's society has made a 'perfect landing' into a transfigured, maladjusted, highly malfunctioning world.

The 'good' that God created for mankind has been transformed by corruptive, damaging, contaminating, dark, deadly worldly pursuits—the world today is 'hellish' sanctioned! All possible hopeful prospects have been eroded. Nonetheless, you can counter the horrific consequences life today presents with a zone of comfort, a spiritual platform for living.

Jesus Christ is a placid, sublime, loving, caring transforming spirit, exactly what's required to reconfigure this highly dysfunctional world.

Is Society today Unhinged?

Has the public become unhinged, operating without thought and reasoning, just plain misguided? Have sensible, reasonable guideposts for living vanished? America and the world seem in the hands of immorality and depravity is the end game total destruction?

You have only to awaken in the morning to find the state of society more destabilized than the day before. Anything goes in our rudderless, dispassionate society. Civility, once commonplace is becoming a thing of the past, plus proper conduct losing to ruthlessness-without cause or reason people are ready to 'strike out' and they prey on others as wild animals might.

Putting it blankly, the conflict between societal norms and reckless change overshadows the United States. (The same could be said about what's happening around the world).

There's no calm world-wide with the uptick of animus, radicalism and violence. The world is rife with eruption and disrupting elements. Where has adherence to goodness gone? Social incompatibility has pushed society into social unrest. We're wading in moral decay. An opposing force seems to have transformed and desensitized our human capacity, sensibilities, and sense of decency, and replaced it with self-absorption, self-aggrandizement and incivility.

Is America Off the Hook?

The recent rise in gun violence disturbs me as no other crime. Across the nation its victims are innocents: from babies to adults, urban centers are dens for 'shootings' with streets marked with the outlines of the young who suffer violent deaths, or are hunched over in wheel chairs like 90-year-old men, maimed for life. How much worse can things become I ask myself hearing about the increasing number of horrific crimes that take place daily? What is causing society to deteriorate, and can we pre-empt moral decay? I trust that what I have just said in no way reflects prejudice or moral judgment. Neither do I want to appear narrow-minded or harsh.

Speaking generally a conversion of a 'looser system of values and mores' in place is responsible for a malfunctioning, declining American society.

A virulent strain has affected society. Something be-devilling has settled over life in America that has nearly destroyed a sense of goodness. Is America off the hook?

This Earthly 'Struggle' is Winnable

Repelling life's challenges is next to impossible without the helping Hand of Jesus Christ. Through his proposal life is reformed and this earthly 'struggle' is winnable.

Society needs to be strengthened by His Glory in these disquieting times. We need the all-knowing God to reign over our lives from that powerful, spiritual, reconciling place. Nothing we do as humans can activate the correction needed for the turbulence we're experiencing. We need the Lord's blessings transferred from heaven. This earthly 'struggle' is winnable.

Life Defined by Christian Principles

As a social observer, I find I'm disappointed about the decadent track America is on. Degrading elements seem to be ravaging a sense of moral decency; a trend toward looser values and attitudes is shifting the culture in the wrong direction. Opiods and other forms of addiction, escalating crime, plus other indicators demonstrate social decline.

Much is going on that adversely affects American society.

For sure, America is in Unfamiliar Territory.

Turn to God, for everything you and your soul need, assume a life defined by Christian principles.

"That Other Better Side"7

Today life is intimidating and uncompromising. Society struggles with adversity, hardship, and all aspects and forms of unmitigated circumstances and issues-we're in warfare with life. Nevertheless, happiness, comfort and a sense of security are not out of reach, for there is that other better side.

As we're struggling more than ever in this hedonistic, unsafe, inglorious, dark world, know that journeying with your brightest light, Jesus Christ is a game changer…it is that other better side.

Our Troubled Young

People, we have a 'problem'...it is with Our Troubled Young!

Something harsh, unforeseen, inglorious, and most of all, heartless and deadly has overpowered, taken over society's children and youth.

As a society we are not prepared for this ground-level experience confronting us with our young. We have an increasing rate of suicide, mental illness among the young is having astounding high numbers; and the use of drugs has escalated, we have rising rates of gun violence and shooting death. Certainly life is difficult for this generation of young people to maneuver. This generation seems suffering from an irrational component, a sense of insecurity, and worst of all, the inability to cope.

You could say young people lack a sound basis for living. In a real sense they are objects of a flawed family structure, ill-prepared for a world ready to pounce, and devour. Today's family structure shows deficits in important areas. Here are some: adequate grounding, sufficient care and attention, dedication to character building, and future preparation. Today, family life is a not the solid, intimate unit; it's less involved, inconsistent, less nurturing, and often without guidelines and guardrails. It's a system that doesn't produce sound reasoning, the ability needed for these hard, untamed, disorganized times.

There are many things reflecting a woefulness encompassing young lives: they feel cast down, as though in the hands of damnation, they feel incapable and feel they are victims of an incorrigible situation—essentially they feel they're facing a totally 'messed up' life.

Something enormous and effective, in the appearance of a social ground swell is necessary for the well-being of the young. Rehabilitation needed, can come through an association with the Lord. He has everything capable of delivering our troubled young.

Life is Not a Holding Pattern, Hanging in the Balance

Is life today in a holding pattern, hanging in the balance? To all of that, I'd say yes, we're in a bewildering, unmovable state that has almost institutionalized society.

This world is in the 'claws' of life—in a woeful, unsustainable, tumultuous hold.

Living under this undeliverable, hostile, dark blanket of bedlam and descent covering mankind and the world, take a moment to experience the seasonal atmosphere God unveils to settle the adverse atmosphere.

We have shown ourselves undeserving of the Lord's favor, nonetheless the Lord God is willing to alter this degrading life system we're in.

Look around at autumn's presentation, the beauty captured in the brilliance and color God has settled over life on earth for mankind's spiritual renewing and revival. You'll come to see His power, and experience life that is not in a holding pattern, hanging in the balance.

The Lord's Healing Presence

In this bleak, incompatible earthly compartment, the Lord's healing presence is ever near, there for you hovering in the atmosphere.

With arms open wide to console, He can lift you from that dark, dark hole. Through injected comforting elements the Lord has spiritual appeal, prepared for the desperate soul He will heal.

The Lord is reaching out to you from heaven above, to align you with His favor and His bountiful love.

In surroundings connecting you with a marvelous, calming essence, you are standing in the brilliant light of the Lord's healing presence.

"The Freed Spirit"

The crush of life pounds my heart, I
seek the living blood and guts
of forsaken love…life's true spirit.
the haunted soul has strayed in areas-antici-
pating the heap and heft of living to come
and conquer all of me, in my desperate
search for the freed spirit.
in experience' corners, I've felt its wealth
and worth, and saw beyond all that it has for me…
before I lose the pearl hailing me with romance
and serenades, I'm wistful elusion is not a fixture,
with discovery joining happiness and
the freed spirit and me.

That Spiritual Place I Have Found

In a disquieting passage in my life, I've been restored by that spiritual place I have found.

From a small beginning I was meant for winning, yet I felt bound.

I'd failed to settle on higher ground, after reaching for it round after round.

The Lord has a habitat, oh so sound, I've been restored by that spiritual place I have found.

That Place with God

A bond with the Lord addresses everything; it makes you capable of handling whatever you're struggling with. For a better life, you need that place with God.

This life journey on earth can seem unmanageable, impossible to maneuver considering all of the dismaying, hurtful, disturbing—the many hardship issues it presents. Nonetheless, there is always help! It is possible to become strengthened against all of life's challenges and wrongs.

I can tell you about a safety net, a glorious, spiritual habitation for your soul giving you Peace, Love, Joy plus everything you need… it is that place with God.

Strengthened Against Adversity

The path of Jesus soothes the soul, His magnificence and brilliance to behold. Spiritual connections quietly center, allowing Bright hope to silently enter. With the presence of the Lord, confusion disappears, something not possible over the troubled years. Righteousness and Blessings God's spiritual light brings, with everlasting hope, His magnified glory rings. As never before salvation you spring to life, made new, something only Christ the Lord could do.

Spiritual awareness God has for us, it's His gift, brightening our lives with incredible calm, the ultimate uplift. Restorative power God alone can afford, if you surrender heart and soul to the Lord. If facing despair, hurt, harm and complexity, with God in all situations you are strengthened against adversity.

Isn't it wonderful that when no one exists to provide what our lives require we are covered anyway? The word "blessing" is another way of saying that the Lord's covering is over us. It's His permanent source which keeps us safe and secure, and free from the harm and danger present in the world. The Lord's blessings are ours for the taking. All that is required of us is that we look to Him for everything, trust Him for everything, and then Praise Him because He is loving, merciful and forgiving; we could never earn the blessings we receive. His love is unconditional. Blessed are we.

Sometimes life puts us in a flood of darkness with perplexing issues. We feel there's no one to turn to who can resolve what's troubling us. The good news, I know someone you can go to and clear away whatever is messing up your life and give you peace and rest. Begin praying and silently wait for the Lord to answer. No matter what it is, God has the help you need, you can rely on the Father for everything. Had I listened to hear God's voice for all of the times I didn't, oh the gains I could have had. His Holy Spirit abides in me, and I am encouraged in my daily life, strengthened against adversity.

My Essay: "Stranded in Life"

The essay Stranded in Life" is an endeavor through poetry, describing the way I feel and see life. In Stranded in Life I retreat to wonderment, fantasy, whimsy as a means to escape the reality of a thick negative, swirling concoction-fear, dissonance, isolation, unworthiness, and disaffection, loneliness affecting me emotionally, spiritually, psychologically, even physically. Stranded in Life uses personification, analogy, allegory, represents a serene, non-judgmental, welcoming retreat that follows the course of my life from ground to sky to the universe, and curls around my vacant soul.

"Stranded in Life" relocated my estranged spirit, my lost soul; it allowed me to engage the gift to channel the universe, the dark depths, the stored away magic and mystery calling him/her to empty the heart and mind into the dark, forlorn forest, the space capsule of life.

From the earliest African American I inherited a sense of history, a story, timing, legacy, a song. I've reasoned that feeling isolated and disconnected in society has a connection to Blacks who walked in paths before me. Following the movement of Blacks from the time of the diaspora until the present, their feeble voice calls from a horrific past; I see their miserable forms from headlights as they tread along life's highway enslaved, rejected, disenfranchised, 'dehumanized'. The poem lays out the truth the misleading aspects of life in the idea that 'nothing warns of life's true difficulties ahead, the past holds a recollection of innocent light, glimpses inside that timid horizon. Wistful and yearning, and sorrow filled, I turn to mystery in a bold atmosphere prepared to hurl at pleasure, to instances recessed in my prior time. The adversarial force idles, while I appeal to the disrespectful goal present in living to Stop', this describing the freed spirit I sought.

Feeling misunderstood and unaccepted, in the poem I address a world view that's viable, a referendum resisting the adversarial, difficult elements in life when I write, 'I hear the plaintive sound, a world's song of woe, a silent cry at dawn burgeoning, carried through the dark day before…the irreversible voice lifting life and worldly burdens from all 'round…keepers of earth's misery, seekers of seasonal relief and calm'.

I assert how life presents its indifference and adversity in the area which says, 'The indefinable adversarial force idles, while I appeal to the disrespectful goal present in living to STOP!' The assertion is also made when I write, 'there are no gleaming horizons, no mountains of certitude, evidenced in dismembered, fractured hopes and dreams. Along with frailty I sit in the pale moonlight, while heavily I cast my eye on life. The crush of life pounds my heart, I seek the living blood and guts of forsaken love…life's true spirit'.

I envisioned life rewarding aspirations and dreams, as exposed in the poem about a town hall I happened upon in Delaware one evening, and became inspired. 'Here, at this site a blade of history seemed to cast its memory into the surrounding's darkened woods. At this location connecting me and the presence of a distant time and place, immense consolation filled me as from a living stream, dream'.

This next extraction from "Stranded in Life" sends the message that life doesn't really offer everything it displays. 'Billboard you glare with promise and sunny invitation pasted and propped in towns and cities. As you stalk urban corners, and lonesome highways, your message is elastic and sometimes somber beyond the picturesque images around hope. A plastic vision in silence, you create dreams in vast surroundings, escorting life scrawled on buildings or plastered signs above wood stilts- alienating forms spreading life's false aspirations through bliss filled messages'.

On sight, objects and buildings, and things have lifted spirit as expressed about sheds, barns, out buildings: ' I'm irrevocably attached to this particular faded tired-looking storage shed, with many windows , of reddish hue…on someone's property, my eyes are pleased to see, although not new.'

Still, another way to explain the lonely, misleading strain life holds is described in this passage of the poem, 'Long, lonely stretches of time install the ground-level experience, pulling back images of life…the peaceful long-haul. The forgotten magical passage, the major movement lies in a soothing, memorable past longing to be loosed from all contractual dejections and disappointments and insecurities. Hope is to take hold of the bargaining chip, the open door to satisfying dreams and peaceful visions- to stare into the prism concocted by the mind, stranded on a walk beside green pastures, walks along lonely streets shaped from misty innocence and uncovered happiness. Mistakenly, over-active imperatives cast a dim view, miss-directing access you'd find in the hunt for joy'.

I might have attempted to incline my way of living according to normal sensibilities, and toward a sense of 'well-being' associated with universal justice, etc., I believe that 'providence' plays a huge role, and I've always conducted my life as a Christian.

A look at a spiritual aspect of my life is poetically described in "Stranded in Life" as follows: 'God is life's reflecting pool, a Spirit of Light…He alone is peace and serenity, a holding ground of joy! He dissolves crushing pain and disperses melancholic strain…the only way out of the slush pile of living. God through His son, Jesus is a leap onto the attainable dream from disconsolation's bank. Stranded where you are, with Him you can saunter to a place of unintended luxury and unexpected tenderness…The Lord God, keeper of significant Brightness, is the Spirit of Light.

A strain of 'hollowness' has vexed me over my lifetime, entrapping my spirit from childhood to marriage, children, grandchildren, other relationships, and other matters. I express those feelings in this section of "Stranded in Life": '

This particular inlet is a desolate, ominous place with unremitting silence, and where the stench of death and decay fills the atmosphere. It is an evening in spring, the time when the Horseshoe crab comes to the Delaware shores to spawn and die

(The Horseshoe crab is a seafaring creature with a spiked head and a tank-like body and resembles a Viking in armor).

The path to the inlet follows a narrow, dirt road flocked by tall, ink-tipped bulrush and sedge through tall fields of wheat, barley and corn. The ancient bodies of the Horseshoe crab cram the inlet's dark, murky waters and the pebbly shores are crowded with their carcasses. (It is a clamorous event with hundreds swimming, and clamoring to join Horseshoe crab that number in the thousands cluttering the stony beach).

A frail wooden pier stands a short distance away in the middle of the dark, active, dramatic waters. (The frail wooden pier seems to be a scale for the desertion of life, a helpless structure there in the passive surreal drape covering the environment of the inlet. Inexplicably, the pier site turns my thoughts to shipwrecks, pirates' coves, coral reefs and even to damask tablecloths').

Today I can say that I feel reasonably safe and secure from harm and danger. Nonetheless, for a very long time fear and depression overwhelmed my life. The dark shadow of death might have begun as early as my childhood. I can remember being fearful for seemingly no reason.

My early childhood took place during the 1940's, 50's in a deeply Christian household in a working class community in Philadelphia, Pennsylvania. As a young girl growing up in inglorious, unrewarding, lowly surroundings, I detached myself and embraced an encouraging outlook. I experienced beacons of light and optimism that guided me to happier pathways. Sometimes it would happen in the simplest ways. The light from lampposts, windows and chandeliers, even automobile lights seemed to enchant me. These and other instances helped me deal with the unpleasant things all around. I suppose inspiring instances kept me from tossing my dreams into an empty horizon. I became determined to use my broad imagination to transform my surroundings, and allow a glorious force to curl around me.

Throughout my life a conveyance of wonder has removed me from negative feelings to a joyful spirit. Perhaps something occurred in childhood that drowned the ability to confront the reality laid before me. Nonetheless, something tender, sentimental and encouraging delivered me to people, places, and even objects and things, and I present my wandering with wanderlust experience in "Stranded in Life"

I've supplied further information in "Coming from The Bottom" that might help explain the poem, "Stranded in Life."

Society Is On a Hellish Path

God's sanctuary on the earth is greatly being ignored today, according to HIS will, word and His way.

Life is unsettled by the detriment it hath, because society is on a hellish path.

Placation surrounds you because God does abide. His Grace lifts from that place He does reside.

With worldly contamination in such high measure, look toward things of the Lord spiritual and softer to treasure.

Guard your heart from what life today hath, because society is on a hellish path.

"Semblances of His Grace, Glory and Supreme Love"

This is a time hosted by darkness, dread, detriment, trials, tumult, tribulation and many other adverse matters-we're living in and contending with a bedeviled, sin-sick world. You might ask what is there you can do about the heaviness of life. I say, sublet your spirit to the 'joy' you'll experience through 'Semblances of His Grace, Glory and Supreme Love'.

Through the calm and peace of His spiritual presentations, the Lord makes available healing and restoration for the distorted, disorienting, complicated, heartless, senseless, disturbing franchise the world has handed over to humankind.

All tenderness and love is confined to God and suspended to you and to everything He has created. (vistas, visions, rolling green pastures, quiet serene moments, instances and locations with picturesque beauty, music, poetry, happy children, adorable animals, streams, rivers, flowers, trees, woods across the way, blue skies, rain, paintings, gardens, murals, mountains, snow-covered roads, forsaken structures submerged in shade and shadows, or grandiose structures brilliant in sunlight, a white picket fence).

Godly solemn, peace-giving spiritual suspensions are what we need nurturing and placating our souls against the many insurmountable, unmanageable, unsettling things harboring our earthly lives.

I say, why not get in touch with the refreshing, breathless wonder of God's spiritually healing presentations—surrender your life to semblances of His Grace, Glory and supreme Love.

PUT THE LORD BACK IN CHARGE

According to Isaiah, chapter 3, verses 1-5:

"For behold, the Lord God of hosts is going to remove from Jeruselem and Judah Both supply and support, the whole supply of bread, And the whole supply of water.

As a social observer, I find I'm disappointed about the decadent tract America is on. Degrading elements seem to be ravaging a sense of moral decency; a trend toward looser values and attitudes is shifting the culture in the wrong direction. Things have gone amuck, and the let's face the truth we cannot bring order to this discombobulated, disjointed society.

Too many have placed life into their hands, out of the Hands of the One who created mankind in His image; the world is suffering from the discord and disarray because society put life on thc 'wrong' path. For certain, the world is not in Good standing, society is no longer on solid ground.

We're in a state of decompression and de-escalation due to the impact of Covid 19, and other major events, nationally and globally that contributed to this damaging, derailing, destructive impact on society. Much is going on adversely causing Americans to feel we're in unfamiliar territory, or as if we're anchored to a millstone.

These 'horrendous' times wiped out pleasures and aspirations and attractions society had manufactured-we now exist in a 'confused mist' of evaporated high hopes and idealistic dreams. We need to turn everything back over to God, let Christian principles define life.

Today life is intimidating and uncompromising. Society strugglcs with adversity, hardship, and all aspects and forms of unmitigated circumstances and issues-we're in warfare with life. Nevertheless, happiness, comfort and a sense of security are not out of reach, for there is that other better side.

As we're struggling more than ever in this hedonistic, unsafe, inglorious, dark world, know that journeying is possible with your brightest light, Jesus Christ, that other better side.

Is life today in a holding pattern, hanging in the balance? To all of that, I'd say yes, we're in a bewildering, unmovable state that has almost institutionalized society.

This world is in the 'claws' of life on earth—it's a woeful, unsustainable, unrecoverable, tumultuous, deleterious society. All of this because we are not deserving of the Lord's favor.

Under this dark blanket of bedlam and descent covering mankind and the world, take a look at a soothing, bright atmosphere God can deliver.

The circumference for normal living has contracted drastically, adversarial elements have upended the kinder experience we had; we've come face to face with a woeful, adversarial, inhospitable, repressive, lethal state of affairs.

Society is in combat with issues surrounding viruses, violence, immorality, the environment, disruption, corruption, injustices, misconduct, and countless other degrading issues. We are a deeply disturbed, discontented, destabilized society. Nonetheless, there is the spirit of hope waiting to help with these complex matters in place.

You might ask, how does mankind conquer this debilitating, disastrous position we can't seem to dismantle? My answer, turn everything over to 'God's Will'! The Lord is all-encompassing, capable of placing our feet on solid ground. Only He has everything we need for this world that is Not in Good Standing.

PEARLS OF WISDOM

If you're living according to the low, raw nature of this world, you're being fooled and greatly short-changed.

For what's 'Best' and 'Right', reach up to the Lord!

"Not Designed for Anxiety and Fear"

Yearning draws me to a dimension joining me with a spiritual place, an inner-sanctum where peace and calm gather around me. Overpowering feelings attach me to hope, inspiration, aspiration, and joy.

The above is an expression of me now, a well-advanced in age writer. However, that was not the way I lived for a very long time. I am a writer who once suffered for a long portion of my life with depression and anxiety attacks.

I am a married mother of three and grandmother to eight, and feeling put together and safe. Nonetheless, I can look back to when we were a military family and depression overwhelmed me. My husband Huey served twenty-three and a half years as a member of the US Air Force.

I have no remembrance as to when or how it all began, but I suffered for years from overwhelming fear, particularly so the fear of death. Somewhere along the way I realized the meaning of the 23rd Psalm and how applied to my life: "The Lord is my Shepherd, I shall not want. He maketh me to lie down in green pastures. He leadeth me beside the still waters. He restoreth my soul. Yea, though I walk through the valley of the shadow of death, I will fear no evil for Thou art with me, thy rod and thy staff, they comfort me."The dark shadow of death might have begun as early as my childhood. I can remember being fearful for seemingly no reason.

My mother loved and served the Lord, and encouraged my siblings and me to be faithful Christians. Her principle instruction was: "Trust in the Lord with all thine heart; and lean not to thine own understanding. In all thy ways acknowledge him, and he shall direct thy paths."' Proverbs 3: 5-6 King James Version

I'd led a very active life at Tyree A.M.E. Church, in Philadelphia, Pennsylvania, my childhood family church. Even so I experienced forms of fear and anxiety that would follow me and escalate in adulthood. After becoming a wife and mother, feelings of despair and depression only deepened as a sinister mass hovering over my life.

"Lord, please don't take me away from my young children and husband and life," I'd often plead in fear of the dark shadow, death holding me captive. No matter where I was the threat of death was always near, ready to lift me up, and carry me away. I could be outside at the clothesline, hanging up diapers and my wash, and become immensely fearful that ominous dark clouds overhead meant that any second God would reach down and snatch me away. I could give account of many frightening episodes I experienced over the years.

"Keeper of my soul rectify me from misdoings, forgive me for transgressions, have mercy," I'd pray every time I encountered terrifying experiences that like movie episodes kept playing. I'd reached a point of feeling that darkness sheltered my life. I was desperate to have the Lord release me from overwhelming fear.

"Loretta, it's time we do something about this problem," my husband Huey insisted one late-evening he became concerned to find me standing in thc doorway of our military housing gazing into the night sky, and heard me asking the Lord to release me from the burden of terror. He insisted I get psychological help.

"What are some of your dark thoughts? The Air Force psychologist asked. I described some of the harrowing experiences. He diagnosed my condition as free-floating anxiety, realizing that I felt anxious about almost everything. Several visits with the psychologist didn't seem alter my condition. I continued living with gloom and doom.

While operating in the military lifestyle it didn't occur to me that I'd divested myself of the way I'd been raised, faithfully serving Christ Jesus. From time to time my family and I went to chapel on bases, and even ventured to some churches off base. However, I wasn't fully involved with Christian fellowship as I grew up doing. The years went on, and I only sank deeper into a field of terror. I worried that at any time death would take me and I'd leave my three children motherless and my husband without me. I'd begun to think that nothing could release me from the dark place where I lived-extreme fear. The saying is true, that you have to reach the bottom before you can change a situation.

Confronted with a medical problem that required surgery, I fearfully thought that going under the knife would seal my fate…everything would end for me on the operating table, or shortly thereafter. After all of the horrifying messages, this was my doomsday. I shook terribly from apprehension as much as from the chilly hospital temperature as an Air Force hospital Corpman wheeled me down the corridor toward surgery. I began praying hard as ever that the Lord would not take this opportunity to fulfill His plan of death. Thankfully, the operation went well. However, while I lay recovering I had a nightmare more terrifying than any experience I'd ever had. In it I'd died and fallen into hell and red devils were painfully stabbing me. In the hardest prayer I'd ever given, I begged the Lord to stop what was happening to me. I couldn't have been more relieved than when my husband woke me from that horrible experience.

That experience showed me something. I began to realize that I needed to follow my mother's message from long ago: "Trust in the Lord with all thine heart; and lean not unto thine own understanding. In all thy ways acknowledge him, and he shall direct thy paths." I realized my relationship with the Lord had become weak, I hadn't followed her advice, and as a result I'd fallen away from the Lord's Will for me.

As soon as I'd regained my health my family and I joined a church, and began serving the Lord. My dependence is on my savior, Jesus Christ. And I can tell you that the more I served Christ Jesus the more the darkness and fear moved away. I now feel safe and secure.

Even as a believer I was spiritually bereft. I hadn't connected responsibly and with total devotion. I hadn't trusted in the living God with all my heart. I wasn't on the path the Lord Jesus Christ and His precious Will had for me. The lights had gone out; I was lost to darkness and fear, and languished in a depressive state. Even though I was raised as a Christian, and continued believing in the Lord into adulthood, evidently I hadn't surrendered everything to him. I'd watered down my dependence on him, my faith needed to be strengthened so I could become whole.

In my opinion God's incredible light is manifested in special experiences He puts in place so that we can witness His renewing of our spirit. I consider them "spiritual guideposts."

I'm now enjoying life because the Lord's incredible Light lifted me out of darkness. My family and I have a fuller, more joyous life because Christ released me from fear.

I consider what I'd experienced was one of Faith finally found... God didn't design me for anxiety and fear.

"His Magnificence"

His magnificence imparts the perfected passage fora fractured humanity!

Move against the irreverent, unholy strains that would pull you from His purpose for this earthly experience.

Trust in the Lord to convert you from this mortal ground to Life eternal.

Believe in the Possibility ground into the Human spirit.

Have Faith, and daily challenge the Cause you represent.

GOD'S TERMS ONLY

Living according to 'God's Terms' confines us to everything fruitful and Good. Everything we He lights the way, puts us on the right path for a better existence on this earth.

The Lord manifests Himself in Three Persons: Father, Son and the Holy Spirit.

Everything is out of our hands, God alone can lift all things burdensome confining you, and make your heart glad.

Put the Lord into your heart through faith and total dependence, and live according to 'God's Terms' only and receive everything possible that's fruitful and good.

"Jesus Christ, a Spirit of Light- Life's 'Perfect Gift'"

Jesus Christ, a spirit of light, life's perfect gift.

God's Son is a reflecting pool of love, peace, joy, comfort, protection.

Jesus Christ is a peaceful dwelling place for crushing pain, a holding ground dispersing melancholic strain, a lifter for darkness covering light's beam to the attainable dream.

The Lord God, Keeper of significant Brightness, Jesus Christ, a spirit of light-life's 'perfect gift'!

Give God Your Hand to Hold

In this unstable, shattered world, make God the Keeper of your soul.

Walk with His Spirit, and Holy Light, Give to Him total control.

You're safe and sound Him by your side, smoother sailing as does a glide.

You've made your life better— enriched, and even bold, if you'll give God your hand to hold.

"Be Enlivened, Christmastime Is Here"

These days it appears we are sealed off from hope and joy by a mass of hardness and darkness that has deeply downgraded our human experience. To this I say, be enlivened, Christmastime is here!

More than ever, the spirit of this world needs the Light of Christ Jesus to counter all of the heaviness pressing against humankind. We are hopeless, weary, misguided travelers for whom He, the Lord can show the way to a hopeful, uncluttered, clear path.

Cheer up! This is a season for regeneration, a time to celebrate the birth of Jesus Christ who brought hope to a fallen world for all of life. Be enlivened, Christmastime is here!

A Perverse Generation

It seems an agenda that discounts a belief in religion is in play in America, one which is particularly averse to Christian doctrine. An extreme cultural shift has landed the country in a decadent tract.

As a Christian growing up in simpler times as I did a sense of moral decency was the norm in America even in the presence of degrading elements in society.

Has the public become unhinged, operating without thought and reasoning, just plain misguided? Have sensible, reasonable guideposts for living vanished? America and the world seem in the hands of immorality and depravity. You have only to awaken in the morning to find the state of society more destabilized than the day before. Anything goes in our rudderless, dispassionate society. Civility, once commonplace is becoming a thing of the past, plus proper conduct losing to ruthlessness-without cause or reason people are ready to 'strike out' and they prey on others as wild animals might. You sometimes have to wonder if total destruction is the endgame.

Putting it blankly, the conflict between societal norms and reckless behavior overshadow the United States. (The same could be said about what's happening around the world).

There's no calm world-wide with the uptick of animus, radicalism and violence. The world is rife with eruption and disrupting elements. Where has adherence to goodness gone? Social incompatibility has pushed society into a state of unrest. We're wading in moral decay. An opposing force seems to have transformed and desensitized human capacity with self-absorption, immorality, self-aggrandizement and incivility.

I sometimes feel lost, separated in a society that's the antithesis of the Christianity that instructed me from early childhood.

I grew up knowing that the Lord's message in the Bible laid the groundwork for the way we should conduct our lives; we feared God's wrath and tried to adhere His word. Everything has so radically changed that I sometimes feel I'm wandering in a chaotic environment that's promoting irresponsible, destructive behavior, a culture totally averse to my Christian belief. I see loose attitudes and a high consumption of decadence trying to overpower the Will of God for earthly beings. Things have veered far from the way God intended.

Christians today are living in a strange land; evil is trying to banish the steadiness and wholeness and nurturing that our spirit requires.

Around the world and across the Nation societies are festering with vulgarities and immorality.

As a Christian I sometimes worry that an inescapable trend is fueling America's demise with the drug and opiod and other forms of addiction, the crime and other signals of social decline. Nonetheless most worrying for me is seeing the broad reach religion once had in America has now greatly diminished, especially so with Christianity.

We need God's Saving Grace to guard against evil's dark force. We must remember the breathless wonder and beauty His magnificent creation emptied into mankind, animals, fowl, seas, spaces, mountains, wilds, towns, everything.

The good news: Spiritual renewal is partitioned behind walls where permanence, grace and love reside…a realm composed of perfection, if we seek the guiding light of God.

A SIN-FILLED PARLOR OF DECEIT

As human beings, we create, remake and reinvent life on earth into a flesh satisfying experience. Nonetheless, a world compacted with pleasure is actually a deleterious den compact with fantasy and trickery, a sin-filled parlor of deceit.

Be consecrated to the Will of God. Let your spirit be absorbed by the Light of Jesus. Turn to the Lord for His loving, comforting, sanctifying presence. Be absolved of the manifestation of worldly pleasure. For everything that's good submit your life to the Lord, seek Him, not damnations' dark presence in 'a sin-filled parlor of deceit'.

"A Glittering Gem, a Small Wonder"

One late-evening in spring I came upon a town hall in rural northern Delaware that impressed me. Standing in magnificence and splendor the Georgian brick structure reached back to the earliest colonists engaged in discussions establishing America. It was like many historic buildings that recapitulate America's Colonial period, represented by Corinthian, Ionic structures, in that it constituted a horrendous revitalizing force.

Though moderate in size, its immense bearing circumscribed its natural origins. Beyond the patriotic significance emanating from the town hall, this municipality amassed by darkness was a gem, a glittering diamond, a small wonder.

Here, a blade of history seemed to cast its memory into the surrounding darkened woods. I felt connected to something spiritual, holy, a living stream at this faraway location. I became aware of a sense of immense consolation filling my spirit.

A BOTTOM FOURTH

My family and I were among the throngs of people returning home from the Fourth of July celebration held in Fairmount Park in Philadelphia, Pennsylvania. We'd spent the day picnicking with relatives, friends and crowds of people. That morning we'd walked the four blocks from Mt. Vernon, the narrow street where my family's row house stood. The Fourth of July was the fulfillment of the summer weeks and days I had spent anticipating it. The day began early with the delicious aroma of fried chicken and the sound of my mother downstairs in the kitchen, preparing an enormous picnic lunch our family would carry to the park. At that very moment, all of my expectations for Independence Day were released.

A blazing, hot day framed thousands of celebrants and Fairmount Park. The exciting day had seen me and others have lots of fun and games and great-tasting foods, and much romping about on the luscious green grounds for which Fairmount Park is exemplary. Even the Fourth of July program that had been echoing throughout the day from a platform across the ocean of enthusiastic picnickers had been entertaining and interesting. On Independence Day the lush, pantheon grounds of Fairmount Park served the public at large in a patriotic sense and in a social context as well. (During all of the levity and celebration, a hallowed, patriotic spirit presided over the surroundings: a permanence and intransigence parlayed and transposed the serene park grounds that a hollow strain inhabited. There were emanations from the American Revolution and from other wars fought in the preservation of our country's freedoms. George Washington's Troops at Valley Forge-Revolutionary War; the War of 1812; Gettysburg; Manassas; Appomattox; the Civil War; the Mexican/American War; the Great War; World War I; Normandy; D-Day-World War II).

The effect of World War II on our community was extensive. My family knew personally men who while fighting in World War II were injured or lost their lives. One very sad case involved a young man, who returned from the war with Japan, hopelessly shell-shocked. Another situation concerned a very notable action on the part of an employer at the factory where my mother worked. It seems that he was one of the three soldiers to place the American flag on the hilltop at Normandy, a brave act indeed. Nevertheless, he contracted a physical condition fighting in the jungles that left him with an incurable odor. A very young mother we knew was left with a toddler to rear alone when her young husband was blown to pieces by German forces. And, of course there were others, some even relatives who courageously contributed to the war efforts of our nation.

I was among my family and others in the park's natural setting. The lush, green floor was fertile ground, reconnecting the past and me. (As I listened, images and transformations of my ancestors hovered over the intimate conversations of my relatives, recreating the source of my background. The experience was comforting, encouraging, and inspiring, even elevating). A long day of excitement ended with the beauty and splendor of fireworks shattering the violet night sky.

Now, the plenteous, fulfilling experience was over and families and others were returning to where they dwelled in the Bottom. I was lost to longing and regret as I stood on the corner at the top of Mt Vernon Street.

A concentration of darkness and gloom saturated the lifeless rummage and plumbing fixture businesses and other businesses at that location. The darkened sky floated with stars and cloudy formations-some of it vestiges of exploded fireworks. A volume of sadness and disappointment infiltrated the darkness magnifying the solemn retraction that normally clung to the Bottom, with the concentration overflowing into Mt. Vernon Street.) With a deep sense of regret and reluctance, I climbed down into the canyon of Mt. Vernon Street. The spectacular, explosive day was over, my spirit and I would have to wait for next year's 'Fourth.'

WICKEDNESS HAS WEAKENED MAN-KIND

The opportunity to fully embrace the promise America purports hasn't happened because of an onslaught of negative elements. A light of hope for a normal society is growing dim. America has increasingly become a defiant, self-rule society; everyone is promoting individuality, pursuing a glorified identity-evil has changed the heart and soul-wickedness has weakened mankind.

It's not inconsequential that when American society abandoned 'values' we experienced dislocation and began falling into decadence; clearly the break-down of the family has aided the social calamity that took hold.

Far too much has been made of a singular approach, the individual pursuit. That angle is the principle reason for the disaster sprawled over American society. The public is playing with a disastrous wild, unstable unsustainable detrimental way of living. Guns and drugs are overwhelming society. The 'inescapable' trend is fueling America's demise.

Is there an agenda with doubt-ridden messages in place powerfully opposing Christian ethics? Americans seem to have released themselves from a Christian perspective, or any belief in God who created everything. Due to extremism, and the fact that individuals have become less unaccountable for their conduct, the culture has shifted in the wrong direction.

For certain an American agenda discounting religion seems in play. Wickedness has weakened mankind.

Loretta Moore, an Advocate for Christ.

"Walk Behind God's Faithful Lead"

With all of the concerns we might have, don't let anything
shut you down, know that Hope is waiting
and desiring to be found.
Place all your Trust in Jesus to help you out….
He's the Answer for all your fear and doubt,
He'll manage all your problems just allow him to take hold…
for then relief is on the way as you He will enfold.
For what you want, and you need, walk behind God's Faithful
Lead.

Tumbling In Life

Life today is in a tumultuous state, it can have you tumbling and spinning as if in a washing machine. Realize that you don't have to remain in that horrific worldly wash and hung out to dry, all of which means you find yourself tumbling in Life.

Know that confronting the vile, unwieldy, disturbing issues commanding this world, there is a 'life-line', Jesus Christ in command over everything, there to rescue, lift you from tumbling in life.

What's Life All About?

Unfortunately, life for real progressed to a point of boldness, yet heavy and without spontaneous relief.

For isn't every living person a victim of idealistic thought, and searching for that bank of prospects and hopefulness that became dislocated and lie somewhere in the belly of shipwrecked dreams, or in the cosmos?

Undergird Yourself with God

With all of the turbulence these days confronting society, you need a strong, sound foundation against the heartaches and defilement the world imposes. The Lord's spiritual, insulating, towering strength is just what is required... undergird yourself with God.

The Way I'm Viewing Life

The human call is enormous looking at everything surrounding life in America and the world.

Thinking about the Covid-19 impact-the 'Monkey Pox' and other disastrous viruses as well-I realized life will never be the same as I observed the regrettable, almost mournful encroachment overlaying the atmosphere these days.

Since the onset of the Corona Virus throughout America and around the world a brisk, hard 'devastating' change has left no stone unturned, no aspect of life untouched. The virus powerfully diminished society's normal relevance as never could have been imagined— it allowed a take-over that defeated the normal societal structure of personal pursuit and self-reliance.

Mankind has rejected the belief that God reigns supreme over His creation, and adopted a lifestyle solely created to satisfy through the spirit of imagination, and asserted a way of life that's fanciful and almost fantasy driven as a reality for the world.

"We Need You, Lord, We Need You, Lord"!

That beautiful Christian song was never more in play and needed than now, with the 'Imposition' and 'Change' Corona Virus has caused! It's especially the case with America, a society so conditioned to having life covered, manageable, a society not accustomed to being overwhelming adversity. We're definitely not designed for the anxiety and fear COVID-19 and other adversarial issues have inflicted. We're in a battle with darkness, but we're beginning to see the light.

My take on the devastating effect of the Corona Virus, Covid-19, and other conditions overpowering society, except for the American

Revolution and the Civil War, nothing America has experienced has been more ' horrific'!

I'm not addressing anything political, or other matters with this piece. My view about this 'dark passage' we're all in is from my perspective.

For certain, something virulent is ravaging society! Coming from a spiritual or religious viewpoint, perhaps the Lord wants us to respect His creation, and demonstrating his dissatisfaction. Regrettably, we are a 'Free Will' society dismissing everything good the Lord presents mankind-'the way, the truth and the life'.

Now, we're beginning to see the light! The human call is enormous!

Americans are experiencing far too many idiomatic impositions, causing society to feel life is more than 'it' can bear.

Has human behavior become too relaxed, and supplanted common decency with reckless, loose conduct?

I'd have to say, Yes, absolutely so. This isn't to say that opposite rigid self-control is the proper conduct, either. Nevertheless, the posture of society today has allowed dereliction of what is sociably acceptable, dutiful, and admissible. The measure for living is reduced to a 'base' level; American society is feeding on the lowest elements for existence.

The country has tossed sane, wholesome platitudes, and reorganized with agendas that promote a twisted, disastrous, counter world view. For certain, American society has lost its simplicity and innocent structure.

In America 'Norms' seem to have fallen by the wayside. Everyone wants to set up his or her personal agenda whatever that is. It can be a personal agenda descending or deleterious-a descent into bedlam is not out of reach

We're living in a time of the power of a 'defilement takeover'.

Decency, morality and solid values have been high-jacked. Far too many Black youth have no idea what a two-parent, religious practicing household is. Too many complications bind them; they feel hopeless in the conditions they find themselves. With no vision or a way to salvage their lives, they grab hold of, or latch on to anything, even to reckless and untoward behavior, things that serve to destroy social standards and a sense of decency: drugs, crime, gangs. The so-called musical form known as Hip Hop or Rap reflects the absence of respect for society and in particular for females and is a reflection of rebellion, and is deleterious. The more outlandish their rap, the better the rappers feel, nonetheless all of it does nothing except to rob them of the true goals of the society about which they create their rap. Some might respond that at least they're making a statement about the horror of their situation. And I say to that, why use harmful, degrading messages that obliterate the standing of decency that use to exist in the community. Why not try advancing measures that improve the conditions of your culture? Haven't depressed societies always strove to dismantle or disassemble or break through entanglements preventing them from advancing in life? Clearly, rappers and hip hoppers send a vile, demeaning message about the Black community.

Violence is ablaze across America, particularly so in Black communities. Certainly it's an environment of despair and crime, a community with little that's positive to draw upon. There is no incentive to imagine or aspire, or to build or rebuild. It seems many have lost hope. As a consequence, everything of lethal or bad consequence exists there: babies born out of wedlock, crime, drugs, and total disregard for authority. There are too many real-life disasters in the African American community and too many too accustomed to living in an environment in which wrong doing is normal. Young women and girls are ill-equipped for the babies they bear; they're having children too early, too young to have any comprehension of how to care for them. One situation I heard about which is not unusual, involves a young woman with no husband, has four small children, one an infant, and all of her children have different fathers. Some in this young woman's predicament are sure to harm their children's futures.

"The U.S. Family Disconnect"

It seems society in America everything began falling apart with the 'breakdown' of the family. As a consequence of fathers absent from the household, families had little to build upon. It's not inconsequential that when American society abandoned 'values' we experienced dislocation, and descent in every area of life today.

For certain, today 'calamity' has wrapped its arms around the American family. Far too much has been made of a singular approach—the 'individual pursuit'. That angle is the principle reason for the disaster sprawling over society. Society is on a disastrous wild, unstable, unsustainable, detrimental course; the path it now follows is disassociated with a sense of decency, and human values.

It is my opinion that a sense of 'togetherness' as the family represents is the optimal way to avoid the catastrophic, disabling impact we see without that familial connectivity.

Seeking His Bountiful Peace

If you have been pursuing a colorful, fanciful, pleasurable worldly style of living the adversary presents, you've lived in a state of default, ignored the truth of life. Nevertheless, God's spiritual domain holds calm, love, and benevolence—a Holy premise perfect for anyone seeking His bountiful peace.

PLEASANT EXISTENCES

I live in the silence of life with pleasant existences.

A place as soft as a flower's petal trails me from trials and confusion to that warm, gracious faraway invitation.

I need no drink or elixir rallying my senses to become capable of fullness and peace.

I'm at that location without prompting, lifted from that arena of animators interpreting an undeliverable, unrewarding, falsified, hapless, base, bedeviled world.

Mankind has fallen to dangerous depths, far distant from a natural, spiritual habitation associated with God, and the experience of pleasant existences.

A Restructured Society

Adaptation after slavery's indoctrination was difficult. Having been deprived of freedom, for so long confined in enslavements rigorous, restricted human construct, Blacks found themselves in convoluted waters on the way to self-discovery and self-identity. They were striking out as lost souls, Black pilgrims. The cruel, oppressive strangle-hold of slavery had co-opted them, their self-worth and human value had long ago retreated leaving them vulnerable and weak and essentially lost. Nonetheless, a spirit of hope was a light on the long, hard, dark freedom's journey.

At the end of enslavement, broadening a since of freedom Blacks abandoned the south in great numbers. They are romantics, adventurers, dark pilgrims clothed in innocence and immaturity, leaving behind the burden of Slavery for a life in the North that's better and promises shelter. Northern-bound, the southerners travel with meager belongings, wrapped in hope and an idealistic dream, with the strength of their projections dented by doubt, and their visions ushered by burgeoning loneliness. Traveling in the summer months means days of relentless, burdensome heat with images of solemn countryside and seas of prolific fields burning in the blazing sun, while the nights swell with the sweet aromas of honeysuckle and magnolia, and the pure magic of soundless, smooth darkness along with the long tracts of landscape looming with mystery and intimidation. Autumn and winter travel present cobalt, somber skies, cold rain and vast vigils of stark, lonesome woods. And, there are the sights of lifeless pasture, and fields stretched by stubble and isolation-the empty fields bore gracious manors, or tiny, tarpaper houses shackled to silent, leaden landscapes. (Making the transfer North was something that would continue).

The system of slavery slaughtered Black humanity, and reassembling the pieces that will make them whole again was never going to be easy.

By the time of the 1940's and 50's Blacks had become reconciled with circumstances of Civil Rights inequity and injustice.

A group of Black leaders arrived on the scene during the 1950's with nurturing, elevating, affirming directives, a time that seemed ripe for the 'stabilizing front' providing leadership. The 1950's period seemed a backdrop of sober hopeful, silent messaging and also ripe with manufactured superficial delightful detractors: televised variety and game shows, picturesque golf courses, camper trailers, and 'rock and roll.' The gates to promise and fulfillment and accessibility began to open, nonetheless it was a time of solid, stark heavy-laden opposition; Negroes knew well their rejected, hidden place in America. It appears, however, that while the heavy dark shadows of injustice and inequality plagued Blacks, the elite amongst them thrived at this point in time.

It was a time notable for a quiet form of activity conducted by Negro leaders. Roy Wilkins, Adam Clayton Powell, Thurgood Marshall, and NAACP, Core, and other organizations formed to strangle the prejudice and racism aimed at preventing Blacks from breathing freedom. These people and organizations served as a coverlet intervening for the harsh, bruising rambling injustice concretely and miserably set before Negroes. This quiet activism settled quietly around the middle-class structure. The gates to promise and fulfillment and accessibility began opening. Nonetheless, the social atmosphere was solid and stark, and heavy-laden with opposition.

This was a time when upper middle-class and middle-class Negroes solidly positioned themselves against injustice and inequality plaguing Blacks; the group of Negro leaders used influence and directives to elevate human rights for minorities.

Wherein the protest movement of the 1960's socially changed the fabric for Blacks seeking to open the doors of freedom in America, with young Whites protesting resulted in social descent. Theirs was a rebellious, ad hoc cause that destabilized, and pulled away America from normal life and civility. They created a revolution that inducted society into upheaval and social demise. The White revolutionary protests lead America polluted norm that introduced free sex, drug use, and other obscene activities. (HIV-AIDS, hepatitis and other health and medical defects the consequence).

Has the public become unhinged, operating without thought and reasoning, just plain misguided? Have sensible, reasonable guideposts for living vanished? America and the world seem in the hands of immorality and depravity is the end game total destruction?

You have only to awaken in the morning to find the state of society more destabilized than the day before. Anything goes in our rudderless, dispassionate society. Civility, once commonplace is becoming a thing of the past, plus proper conduct losing to ruthlessness-without cause or reason people are ready to 'strike out' and they prey on others as wild animals might.

Putting it blankly, the conflict between societal norms and reckless change overshadow the United States. (The same could be said about what's happening around the world).

There's no calm world-wide with the uptick of animus, radicalism and violence. The world is rife with eruption and disrupting elements. Where has adherence to goodness gone? Social incompatibility has pushed society into social unrest. We're wading in moral decay. An opposing force seems to have transformed and desensitized our human capacity, sensibilities, and sense of decency, and replaced it with self-absorption, self-aggrandizement and incivility.

The African American community has become a place of disdain for what is right, and standards; a sense of morality and values have fallen remarkable low, the reason for a cursed bedlam known as 'The Hood.'

When my thoughts turn to what's going on with young people in American society I see a decline in standards a 'digital' component has aided. It seems a renegade spirit has taken over. My worst impression of youth today involves young males wearing their pants low. First of all the sight of young men with their pants hanging off of their behinds contributes to public discomfort. Secondly, it's a ridiculous sight when they lift their pants to avoid tripping, looking as if to curtsey. Generally speaking, the values my parents taught me have slipped away. Something seems to have eroded the mores of earlier generations. And clearly, they worked so hard to bring us out of our African American historical baggage. First enslavement, then a time when injustice ruled with Jim Crow period with a mandate known as, 'Sundown laws' threatening any Black caught in the town after the sun went down that he could be lynched. Regrettably, the Sundown laws affected one of my relatives.

Decency, morality and solid values have been high-jacked.

Far too many Black youth have no idea what a two-parent, religious practicing household is. Too many complications bind them; they feel hopeless in the conditions they find themselves. With no vision or a way to salvage their lives, they grab hold of, or latch on to anything, even to reckless and untoward behavior, things that serve to destroy social standards and a sense of decency: drugs, crime, gangs. The so-called musical form known as Hip Hop or Rap reflects the absence of respect for society and in particular for females and is a reflection of rebellion, and is deleterious. The more outlandish their rap, the better the rappers feel, nonetheless all of it does nothing except to rob them of the true goals of the society about which they create their rap. Some might respond that at least they're making a statement about the horror of their situation. And I say to that, why use harmful, deleterious messages that obliterate the standing of decency that use to exist in the community. Why not try advancing measures that improve the conditions of your culture? Haven't depressed societies always strove to dismantle or disassemble or break through entanglements preventing them from advancing in life? Clearly, rappers and hip hoppers send a vile, demeaning message about the Black community. Certainly, it's an environment of despair and crime, a community with little that's positive to draw upon. There is no incentive to imagine or aspire, or to build or rebuild. It seems many have lost hope. As a consequence, everything of lethal or bad consequence exists there: babies born out of wedlock, crime, drugs, and total disregard for authority. There are too many real-life disasters in the African American community and too many too accustomed to living in an environment in which wrong doing is normal. Young women and girls are ill-equipped for the babies they bear. They're having children too early, too young to have any comprehension of how to care for them. One situation I heard about which is not unusual, involves a young woman with no husband, has four small children, one an infant, and all of her children have different fathers. Some in this young woman's predicament are sure to harm their children's futures.

Dr. Martin Luther King Jr. intended to establish a just place for African Americans in society. We lifted ourselves from the injustices of the past and attained rights equal with everyone else in America. You have young African American men of today incarcerated at an incredibly high rate. In essence they become a silent majority essentially, an unaccountable segment, barely contributing part of society: not in the work force, not maintaining the family structure- not available even for family procreation.

Why have many Black males that have shifted to risky and criminal behavior. I'll try to bring up some of the causes for this horrific condition in which the Black male finds himself. It all goes to the uninspiring, poor, negative environment where they live. They see little to nothing in their midst to give them the initiative to lead productive lives. Drugs and blatant criminal activity in the community act as a lure. They grow up in homes where they don't receive proper attention and nutrition, education, everything necessary for developing physically, emotionally, and with the skills or competency society requires. In conclusion, everything adds up as an improbable situation for Black males. Perhaps with some understanding, we can think of Black males sauntering about wearing low pants as a superficial means to boost their low self-worth.

The high rate of arrests for petty or low-level offenses might account for some of the huge numbers of African America males in prisons across the country. Removing them from society and handing out long sentences for having an insignificant amount of marijuana helped serve to break up the family structure. It becomes less and less possible to have households with a mother and a father. The irrational, immoral behavior that involves sharing paraphernalia infected with HIV-AID's also accounts for the way the horrific disease is spread.

The recent rise in gun violence disturbs me as no other crime. Across the nation its victims are innocents: from babies to adults, urban centers are dens for 'shootings' with streets marked with the outlines of the young who suffer violent deaths, or maimed are hunched over in wheel chairs like 90-year-old men. How much worse can things become I ask myself hearing about the increasing number of horrific crimes that take place daily? What is causing society to deteriorate, and can we pre-empt moral decay? I trust that what I have just said in no way reflects prejudice or moral judgment. Neither do I want to appear narrow-minded or harsh.

Speaking generally, a conversion of looser system of values and mores in place is responsible for a malfunctioning, declining American society.

A virulent strain has affected American society. Something be-devilling has settled over life in America that has nearly destroyed of a sense of goodness. Is America off the hook?

Societal displacement has led to world chaos and a sense of disaster and doom. Normalcy is not valued the way it used to be. But neither is self-governing playing a role in our lives. We do what we want without regard to what it is we are following. Put blankly, we are a lost tribe around the world.

Where in the past have you seen such desolation and depravity? Speaking generally, the public is unhinged and without thought and reasoning, just plain mean! There have always been guideposts for reasonable living, and they still exist. Immorality is breaking down America and destroying the world: You have only to awaken in the morning to find the state of society more destabilized than the day before. Anything goes in our rudderless, dispassionate society. Civility is a lost art, and ruthlessness commonplace.

Without cause or reason people are ready to 'strike out'-they prey on others as wild animals might.

Society is in desperate need of Restructuring!

Jesus, and Our Salvation

Earthly beings, problem free, never! At some time in life all of us will deal with heartache, disappointment, tragedy, disagreement, death, ill-health, division, loneliness and emptiness, rejection, and countless other kinds of misery living on earth poses. A devoted friend is nice to turn to when we are confronted by any of these issues. However, even if you have that kind of treasured friend, the time can come when the best companion can't assist you. Just imagine a friend capable of handling every kind of problem, the unthinkable included. Well, I know Jesus Christ, and He is that friend. He's always around; He will never let you down. The way to Him is through faith.

I truly believe that Jesus Christ is the basis for our strength on this earth. He's the armor against all adversity. You cannot match His love and devotion with anyone's, anywhere. Jesus Christ is a friend in need; a friend indeed.

The Birth of Jesus is the Heavenly Father's most important gift to the world. Look at all of the marvelous things that embody life—the sun, moon, the universe. No gift compares to God's only Son. Without Jesus Christ human beings would find the conditions of life empty, disappointing, devastating, and worse. We were pressed low until the birth of Jesus made us recipients of His precious light. We are one of God's gifts.

We have become new, better human beings because of the Holy One, Jesus Christ, the Son of God.

Much is Lacking this Harvest Time

Thanksgiving is approaching in an atmosphere that's less than abundant and bountiful this year—a dimming spirit hovers over the usual gatherings at tables across America because much is lacking this harvest time. Complexity, rough and disheartening times abound, covering every front this autumn season. Generally speaking, due to an overwhelming decrease in the normal abundance associated with Thanksgiving, American society finds itself stilted, almost paralyzed.

Looking at the impact of the 'pandemic' specifically this Thanksgiving, insufficient provisions and undeliverable supplies challenge and diminish the usual 'bountiful' season. (Thankfully, 'vaccinations' have tapped down last year's Covid 19's and variants' deleterious impact).

As we observe a landscape across America harboring autumns' appeal of plum, orange, red, vibrant colors, we find Thanksgiving 'fractured'. Nonetheless the All loving, giving Lord, God is 'sufficient' for everything this season and all seasons, even though it appears much is lacking this harvest time.

This Year, 2022

As 'Thanksgiving' has arrived, and these are formidable times still-life is not available in plentiful and bountiful measure- we can Praise the Lord for bringing us to a better place.

We have to Thank the Lord for 'hope' and 'relief', His Blessed Assurance!

No Substitute for God

God is a placid, reviving perfect heavenly plain, and Only He is capable of lifting you from all things unfavorable, disturbing, devaluing, incurable, horrific, deadly impacting life. The truth, there is 'No Substitute for God'.

This wretched, vile, reckless, scattered society appears totally out of the will, way, and love of God, rejecting the 'good' as put forth by His Saving Grace', for the 'worst' this world proffers.

The Lord God represents the Highest, the Best, He is Perfection that no placebo, intervener, interpretation can supplant. He is 'The Great I Am', 'The Almighty', 'Savior of the World', indisputably, there is 'No Substitute for God'.

His Holy, Holy Presence

Life is embedded with much disrespect and much travail, and we're a society bruised, battered from worldly assail.

In a perilous, ravaged world where dark, dark times prevail, we wait in need of 'help' and 'hope', all to no avail.

The world is spinning with many earth-shattering things contracting life, while silence and stagnation hover in this atmosphere; life today is 'boundless' looking at the difficult things society has to endure. (An incredible wave of crime is heavily incapacitating the normal course of life—it's an impostor, a hostile dynamic stealing, slaughtering our young and youth).

In these times for a world of decadence, we need to call on the Lord God to install from heaven a certified cure-all, 'His Holy, Holy Presence'.

EMBRACE THE LORD, AS YOUR SAVIOR

Society presents life flourishing and appealing, however what it is presenting is a vision, an illusion. In truth, the world is fraught with trouble and suffering, it is your adversary.

An 'enormous threat' is everywhere, no place is 'unavailable' to the hard, unconscionable, troubling, constraining, deadly doings penetrating life. Nonetheless, you can be delivered from what this 'world' proffers if you'll embrace the Lord as your savior.

Repelling life's challenges is next to impossible without the helping Hand of Jesus Christ. Through his proposal life is reformed, and this earthly 'struggle' is winnable.

Society needs to be strengthened by His Glory in these disquieting times. We need the all-knowing God to reign over our lives from that powerful, spiritual, reconciling place. Nothing we do as humans can activate the correction needed for the turbulence we're experiencing. We need the Lord's blessings transferred from heaven.

The world needs to be strengthened by His Glory. Embrace the

Lord as your savior!

You Will Never Have It All

You will never have it 'ALL' on this earthly plain.

A happy and full life you cannot attain,

With the Lord alone comes 'ALL' to sustain.

Do Not let the World Get You Down

Shade and shadows might have overtaken the landscape, and we're experiencing the heaviness of life, but do not let the world get you down.

In a spiritual vein, a dark, unholy force stalks life. Nevertheless, beyond this dominant miserable situation, the Lord Jesus with open arms stands waiting with vast hope for mankind's survival and renewal—with the Lord life is manifold and

Great!

Do not let the world get you down.

This Wretched, Scattered Society

This wretched, scattered society is misplaced, having put everything outside of the love of God. A connection with human values and decent attributes appears removed from society—something reckless, irresponsible, and vile has perpetrated human nature taking society totally out of control. The world today is a 'horrific' place with all that is ravaging life.

Restored faith in the Lord is the only Hope for this wretched, scattered society.

"Jesus Christ for a Lifeline"

Society world-wide is not in a safe place. The world doesn't present what is best for mankind. However, Jesus Christ is our Lifeline.

Life has humankind tumbling in a washing machine, or in an erupting volcano, or in flood waters, or a tsunami being bashed about and/or overtaken or consumed by raging fires...I could go on and on speaking about this 'horrific' earthly experience.

The world with everything it presents can never be in a position to offer what is best for society. In truth, humankind needs to take hold of Jesus Christ for a lifeline.

Just Come Out of this World

In the face of a devastating, unconquerable, overpowering, unrewarding experience life presents, the love of God is available if you'll just come out of this world.

We as earthly beings have rejected a sound spiritual-directed bond with the Lord God and have attached ourselves to the indecency and wiles that prevail in the world. We seem to have forgotten that the Lord's intensions are the best for us, 'the way, the truth, and the life'!

Society has been drained of sound reasoning, and co-opted by a vile, violent response. The public no longer responds to a' moral compass', and the term, 'the common good' no longer applies-ruthlessness, self-direction, and self-indulgence represent the normal modes of conduct. Generally speaking, an intransigent 'hardness' now occupies our hollowed-out souls.

Without Jesus Christ, Son of God in control you're on a lonely trail dealing with instability, desperation and suffering.

If you desire to be loosed from the havoc, discord, heaviness, and dastardly elements stalled over life, turn to God, be consumed by His Love, just come out of this world.

Troubling Times

As a Christian and a writer, I'm moved to address today's 'troubling' times!

The horrific violence perpetrated on life is incredible, and most of it can be attributed to our 'Youth'. As such I've begun creating Videos of my 'inspirational Christian writings' and posting them on 'Tik Tok,', 'Instagram', and other social online platforms where the young are. Today's youth are caught up in this deleterious, hard, wicked world to which they've been unbelievably exposed. (For that I blame 'environment' and 'insufficient parenting'). Most of the young have 'never' been introduced to the 'Goodness' of the Lord God, the Saving Grace of Jesus Christ. As such I hope to somehow alter the 'wiles' of the world influence on society, using my work as a Christian writer, doing Videos and presenting them on 'Tik Tok', 'Instagram', and all other Online Platforms where the young go.

I hope and pray that my 'Videos' will change the young by introducing them to God, who with His 'Goodness' can turn them away from their involvement with the wicked world, and rekindle, rejuvenate their lives.

The Hellish World We Inhabit

I was moved today by the horrendous news about the shooting in Texas at that elementary school...this should Not be happening!

I'm sharing another video expressing my feelings as a Christian writer. The public needs to turn to God, away from this corruptible, hellish world we inhabit.

I'm particularly interested in the 'Youth' in America and their involvement with the horrific state of things-gun violence in particular.

My thoughts on the young and the waywardness, crime, drugs, and shootings, and other things eroding life in America, shows 'un-Godliness' as the cause!

Parents no longer introduce children to the Lord Jesus. As such, they're open only to this wicked 'world' and the deviation, perversion, all of the ugliness it presents. The young need to know that God created life on earth to be Good, and they the 'youth', and everyone needs to release themselves to Him.

I'm posting this and all of my videos on 'tik Tok'-where the young really are, hoping and praying that what I relate as a Christian writer will touch hearts and connect them with the Lord!

IT'S ON HIM YOU NEED TO CALL

We are lost hosts wandering in a wilderness of adversity and uncertainly. As a society we're confused, destabilized, over-burdened—floundering in this upended world. Nonetheless, Jesus Christ has it all, it's on Him you need to call.

Don't be convinced that an uneven, perplexing, wrong path has you in its hold, because the Lord is a 'leveler' for what's so hard and bold.

If fear taunts you that you will fail or fall, it is on Him you need to call.

Here I am old me, once more doing something new!

This time I'm venturing into territory that's way beyond what I've ever done, creatively. I'm thinking about creating a 'Podcast' that will represent or be comprised of almost all of my creativity-poems, songs, musicianship, singing, plays, short stories, essays, extracts from my novels, inspirational writings and more.

I'm saying all of this because for me do this, I'm going to need an audience.

So, when you see one of my 'presentations' from this 'Podcast', I'm asking that you leave a comment for it.

Thank You So Much for your Support for this old Writer!

Old Me, and a Podcast

Here I am old me, once more doing something new!

This time I'm venturing into territory that's way beyond what I've ever done, creatively. I'm thinking about creating a 'Podcast' that will represent or be comprised of almost all of my creativity-poems, songs, musicianship, singing, plays, short stories, essays, extracts from my novels, inspirational writings and more.

I'm saying all of this because for me do this, I'm going to need an audience.

So, when you see one of my 'presentations' from this 'Podcast', I'm asking that you leave a comment for it.

Thank You So Much for your Support for this old Writer!

Living with His Spiritual Light

Society is confronting loneliness, disaffection, and chaos and worse due to a hard, dark, unfathomable place assigned to the world these days.

With Jesus Christ and His embrace, all of your 'troubles' are covered because you're living with His spiritual Light.

The Lord God, a Righteous Deliverer

We're living in a world compact with 'unrighteousness'; society today is on a path harboring deception, adversity, disillusionment, ill-will, waywardness, unhappiness, destruction, Death. Nonetheless, there is hope for life on earth— the Lord God is a Righteous Deliverer!

Know that spiritual enhancement comes from the Lord God, a Righteous Deliverer capable of destroying Satan, the betrayer, slayer and his evil threat to the world.

Put another way, it's a huge mistake trusting a world of provocation, disturbance, fault and failure- the uttermost destruction.

We don't have to stand alone, confused, suffering, struggling, and afraid in this enormous wickedness and darkness overspreading life. The spirit of the Living God is a beautiful welcoming lighted path to tread, and be extricated, elevated, saved. The savior for all that's wrong and unrighteous in this world is the Lord God, a Righteous Deliverer!

This Wretched, Scattered Society

This wretched, scattered society is misplaced, having put everything outside of the love of God. A connection with human values and decent attributes appears removed from society—something reckless, irresponsible, and vile has perpetrated human nature taking society totally out of control. The world today is a 'horrific' place with all that is ravaging life.

Restored faith in the Lord is the only Hope for this wretched, scattered society.

Jesus Christ for a Lifeline

Society world-wide is not in a safe place. The world doesn't present what is best for mankind. However, Jesus Christ is our Lifeline.

Life has humankind tumbling in a washing machine, or in an erupting volcano, or in flood waters, or a tsunami being bashed about and/or overtaken or consumed by raging fires...I could go on and on speaking about this 'horrific' earthly experience.

The world with everything it presents can never be in a position to offer what is best for society. In truth, humankind needs to take hold of Jesus Christ for a lifeline.

His Light of Hope Still Shines

A dark phase seems in position over the world comprised of wars, confusion, fear, disappointment, disease, and more. Society is held captive and it appears nothing is available to help break away from this vengeful tract we're in.

Christ Jesus can disarm this horrible worldly attack and dissolve this evil darkness hosting life. Know that we can be reconciled, become whole because His light of Hope still shines.

Spiritual Beings

Regrettably, the way that society operates seems to be everything except representative of 'good-will', and a 'higher, 'better' form of life we'd have as 'spiritual beings'!

Speaking of Americans in particular, we have become dispositioned, desensitized, frivolous, self-indulgent, and as a consequence experiencing all kinds of ill-will the world has transmitted to our lives: failure, falling, detriment, disaster.

(Due to our fragile, self-appeasing human nature the dark world has taken command and we're forfeiting everything 'good' that's possible for life on earth.) Our true purpose and pursuit come solely under the Grace and Will of God and His Son Christ Jesus.

For a life lighter, brighter and fuller, give the Lord your mind, heart, and soul for the enormous benefits guaranteed when you're one of His 'spiritual beings'.

Inch by Inch

Inch by inch, little by little, Blacks have had to make their way toward equal status in America.

With God our helper, in a landscape cluttered with hostility, opposition and uncertain acceptance, African Americans plowed their way through and moved ahead.

From Slavery to Jim Crow and discrimination in various forms- some subtle, some overt, reaching the ultimate 're-humanization' goal has been accomplished, almost.

With all of my soul I seek 'total reformation' and to be fully embraced. Whenever it occurs, filled with rapture

my life shall be.

Be Strengthened by His Glory

Society needs to be strengthened by His Glory in these disquieting times. We need the all-knowing God to reign over our lives from that powerful, spiritual, reconciling place. Nothing we do as humans can activate the correction needed. We need the Lord's blessings transferred from heaven to counter the dismay, turbulence, and joylessness we're experiencing.

The world needs to be strengthened by His Glory.

This Darkened Horizon

On this day with splashes of snow and disturbing cold, life is more so about a concentration of 'disheartening' issues across the land—this darkened horizon.

Although this shaft of overpowering darkness is 'discomforting', it is not cause for despair—the Light of Christ Jesus is a 'Lifter' for this darkened horizon!

Praying for a Happy, Blessed 2022 for Everyone!

I'm Thankful to the Lord for bringing my family, and others through the past year, and 'hopeful' about the promise 2022 holds.

I'd now like to comment on the regions' heavy snowfall as a writer: There is the sense that nature has sprawled magic across the snowy landscape!

Now to sharing some great news '2022' has brought to my writing life:

Beginning last year, 2021 in the month of December, our daughter, Lalani asked Huey and me to share with her and our children and grandchildren by writing about our lives. This would be done through STORY WORTH, a popular publisher that does legacy- type books for parents and grandparents and such!

Huey and I every Monday morning for a year, would answer questions Lalani had for us. We ended the book about us in early December, and oh boy, "A COLLECTION OF LIFE STORIES" by Huey and Loretta Moore was a project that turned out to be quite 'pleasing'.

Now to something else I'm Thankful for:

I have a book of poems that just came out titled, "SIXTY POEMS" that I'm hoping you'll want to purchase and enjoy!!!

I'll provide more information real soon!

Thank you all for allowing me to share my writing life.

TOTAL RESTORATION

We're on an indefinable, uncertain, adversarial Journey. It almost seems we're being held captive by an onslaught of plaguing, brutal issues subtracting from our fullest experience-for certain possible joy has been put on hold.

Only 'Jesus Christ' can keep us from succumbing to this wretched journey we're on. A path of 'Total Restoration' comes Only through recognizing Him, and His Love for us.

WE'RE NOT ALONE

In our desperation, Lord put us on the path of your Grace and Mercy. We are lost without You, Lord. Help us to challenge the disabling, adverse forces crippling our lives. Show us the way to Your Light that shines before this darkened wall of life.

Lord, you are at the core of my being, revive my soul, lead me to Hope eternal and Peace that rests in You alone.

Jesus Christ, a Spirit of Light- Life's 'Perfect Gift'

Jesus Christ, a spirit of light, life's perfect gift.

God's Son is a reflecting pool of love, peace, joy, comfort, protection.

Jesus Christ is a peaceful dwelling place for crushing pain, a holding ground dispersing melancholic strain, a lifter of darkness covering Lights' beam to the attainable dream.

The Lord God, Keeper of significant Brightness, Jesus Christ, a spirit of light-life's 'perfect gift'!

This World is NOT in Good Standing

The world is not in good standing, society is no longer on solid ground. The circumference for normal living has contracted drastically, adversarial elements have upended the experience we had; we've come face to face with a woeful, adversarial, inhospitable, repressive, lethal state of affairs.

Society is in combat with issues surrounding viruses, violence, immorality, the environment, disruption, corruption, injustices, misconduct, and countless other degrading issues.

We exist beneath an overwhelming dark cover that seems unremovable and unresolvable; it seems we've been disinherited by the former steady lifestyle that was settled over life. We are a deeply disturbed, discontented, destabilized society. Nonetheless, there is the spirit of hope waiting to help with these complex matters of life in place.

You might ask, how does mankind conquer this debilitating, disastrous position we can't seem to dismantle? My answer, turn everything over to 'God's Will' for mankind. The Lord is all-encompassing, capable of placing our feet on solid ground. Only He has everything we need for this world that is Not in Good Standing.

Written By My Daughter, Lalani

I've been quite silent for a while now. Somewhat caught in my own head. I'm in a place of reflection and introspection. In this time I think about what I am grateful for and during my run today, two people came to mind, my mother and my mother-in-law, both of whom are phenomenal women.

Mom, words cannot express how proud I am to be your daughter. You are an incredible, caring, kind, creative, eccentric and beautiful person inside and out. You have been my rock, my comedian and my guide with our Wednesday check in calls. You have made me into the writer that I am through your years of correcting my papers and articles throughout school (lots of tears then though) and I will forever be indebted to you for helping me discover my gift and profession. And you have demonstrated and taught me perseverance and resilience in life in more ways than you'll ever know. You are a talented writer, an amazing musician and an all around good person and I want you to know that I love you and that you are special to me.

Bernadette, I tell everyone that I have the best mother in law that anyone can ever have. To me you truly are my second mom and I don't know what I would do without you. You are generous, kind, funny, direct and opinionated with good intentions, and you're an incredible "maga" for Mason and Walker. I greatly appreciate you and all that you do and like my biological mom, I love you too!

Thank you both for being such phenomenal women!

Hope Lures Across Life's Landscape

Even in this season when the surroundings display autumn 's color and brilliance, society is held captive by a dark, debilitating, heavy, draining, disastrous spirit. However, in this autumnal landscape, hope lures.

In view of a colorful palette, I sublet my spirit to silent, arresting beauty on this autumn day. And in the presence of nature, and God's Glorious Light hope lures across life's landscape.

Abomination Has Brought us to this Horrific State of Affairs

As a Nation and globally, we're experiencing 'Horrific' times attributable to our rebellious, self-absorbed, sinful, worldly pursuit—frankly speaking, 'Abomination!

As a society we've gone against God's proscription for our lives, replacing it with our own reasoning and self-governance and will, all of which have caused the strain and struggles, and dissatisfaction, the absolute decline with life we confront—this overwhelming dark, heavy earthly position constricting us!

What can we do to reposition our lives to higher ground, turn things around? My suggestion, make a pact with the Lord, realizing that He is overall, allow His love for us to overturn the 'Abomination' that has brought us to this Horrific state of affairs!

Has The World Turned Against Us?

I'd have to answer, 'YES' to the question, "Has The World Turned Against Us?"

With all of the complex, devaluing, disastrous, destabilizing issues transforming life, we're having to endure, causing life to feel unmanageable and almost unlivable, there's no other way to view life, except that 'the world has turned against us'.

The invasion of the COVID and its Variants, the alarming Violence, the natural disasters happening everywhere, society's immoral, perverted direction, the general sense of dislocation impacting society, the 'break-down' of the family and other systems of social conduct, and add to that the recent scare of the 'murder bees' , clearly the world has turned against us.

As I always do with my 'writing's', I offer a 'restorative message' that can retrieve a spirit of calm we've lost to this 'worldly assault'. That advice is turn to 'Jesus Christ', solely place your life in the Hands' of the Lord to turn Everything back to a 'zone of comfort' the world has stolen.

What a Grand Purpose, Life

Send complexities and difficulties
away to a distant shore.
Gods' tender, consoling spirit can enrich your being
fully.
Then no havoc can invade to collect your soul.
Serve a solid motive aligned with His love and
peace.
Don't be conformed to the destruction and cruelty
living presents.
Be lifted through the Lord's offering of 'goodness',
then what a Grand Purpose, Life!

An Inspirational Verse

Life can appear to flower with elements
of the enemy targeting you…
However, look to God during every
overriding Tide…early, turn to Him for
that safe, secure Side…
When you know Jesus
Hope comes shining through…
When you know Jesus
He will tell you what to do…
When you know Jesus
The Way He'll show to you…
When you know Jesus, the spirit of life becomes True.

LOSE YOURSELF TO GOD

We sometimes feel overwhelmed by life, I know I do. And in those troubling times, if I didn't know the Lord I would become a victim of despair and depression.

I am guaranteed help for all my troubles because I believe in Jesus Christ, God's only Son. Through the Holy Spirit, all my worries are vanquished. With Him we can work through our trials when we are challenged, He is in charge of All things.

No matter how deeply-troubled you are, remember, your Deep Faith translates into His Peace.

Solidarity with the Lord

Calamity seems on our doorstep! Life is over-flowing with disaster and detriment. We're perplexed, confounded in hostile surroundings. We're living in a chaotic, malfunctioning world.

What I've mentioned, and more applies to life today.

Has mankind stretched a bridge too far? Have our miss-calculated actions caused the horrific, harrowing experience through which we're having to solemnly walk? Who knows!

I know about a 'Shelter' for atrocities and suffering of all kind you can claim— 'Solidarity with the Lord'!

COVID and VARIANTS

COVID and VARIANTS are calling the shots for America and the world...admit it!!!

Nonetheless, we can Call on the Lord who holds everything in His Hands to reprise us from this brutal force against mankind. The all-encompassing Lord is capable of altering any and everything. With Him as your Keeper, you won't have to live on a blade of hope, complexed in this dark, dark world. Everything becomes 'lighter', 'better' with the Devine Love of God over your life.

A CHANGE NEEDED

Looking around at the disappointment, fraudulence, artifice the 'world' has structured over life to 'appease', we need change!!!

The Lord alone is the perfect, glorious 'Change' we need for these, confounding, challenging, unrewarding times!!!

Has The World Turned Against Us?

I'd have to answer, 'YES' to the question, "Has The World Turned Against Us?"

With all of the complex, devaluing, disastrous, destabilizing issues transforming life, we're having to endure, causing life to feel unmanageable and almost unlivable, there's no other way to view life, except that 'the world has turned against us'.

The invasion of the COVID and its Variants, the alarming Violence, the natural disasters happening everywhere, society's immoral, perverted direction, the general sense of dislocation impacting society, the 'break-down' of the family and other systems of social conduct, and add to that the recent scare of the 'murder bees' , clearly the world has turned against us.

As I always do with my 'writing's', I offer a 'restorative message' that can retrieve a spirit of calm we've lost to this 'worldly assault'. That advice is turn to 'Jesus Christ', solely place your life in the Hands' of the Lord to turn Everything back to a 'zone of comfort' the world has stolen.

SPIRITUAL RENEWAL

In this social upheaval, the normal structure around life, the steadiness and wholeness we'd grown to know has been driven away. Many things have veered far from the way God intended and America is festering with vulgarities and immorality and fractured souls. As a Christian in this world of woe, it feels as if we're living in a 'Strange land'.

The good news is that a Spiritual renewal is possible if society can strive to reconnect with the perfect, guiding light of God that partitioned place, that place of Peace where His Grace and permanence resides.

The Way of the World Disorients and Entangles

Following the way of the world portends a true sense of freedom. A free-wheeling, non-conforming lifestyle makes everything and anything appear good and accessible. Living through exploits and exploration, being unaccountable, subjects mankind to what is wrong—the way of the world 'disorients' and 'entangles'. It's truthfully an unsafe, unrewarding, and possibly disastrous path to be on.

Play it safe and sound, get on the Glorious, Righteous path following the Lord.

Sharing a Message on FAITH, My FAITH!!!

Today, as with each and every day, I realize the Value of my FAITH in the Lord.

God's presence in my life grows I know that with HIM I'm in a safe and secure place.

My Faith in Christ Jesus has shown me that the world is filled with distortions and variations, things destructive and absolutely Contrary to the 'Beneficent' path I have with God accompanying my Walk.

I treasure my Growing 'FAITH' in the Lord.

Honoring Fathers

Today, with Father's Day is approaching, and there is so much to say as 'Fathers' are so important to the structure of family life, and should be '\Honored' in more ways than can be imagined, I begin that 'Incredible Admiration'.

First of all, I praise 'GOD', Father of all mankind!

Next, I honor William R. Butler, my deceased earthly father.

Following the Lord Most High, and my earthly father I honor my husband, Huey Moore, 'father' of our children.

I honor our son Vernon Ladon Moore, a marvelous, Christian father.

I honor our son Lester Dean Moore, a marvelous, Christian father.

I honor our son-in-law Dr. Steve Perry, a marvelous, Christian father.

Over time I'll follow with pictures and images representing these men who are Fathers that I so highly Value!

Today, I'm sharing two of my 'Inspirational' writings

America needs the Love of God to transform the 'human spirit' in the face of the rampant violence we're experiencing. We're becoming a nation of virtual 'warfare enemies'! This violent streak has to Stop!

"Consoled"

I am consoled by sentimental points and places seizing me, delivering me to tenderness never experienced or felt. I never realized pleasant appealing pastures or commanding passage before now. In the silence of buried possibilities and passion I was Everyman seeking to remedy the answer to the soulless portion living deep inside-prepared to heave regret and fear into a loveless, sound-proof background.

Don't expect for anything on the wings of life to blow against winds of enormous universal sources and factors.

Sojourn with God, and His Son Jesus, let them Light the way through this darkened, unconquerable, earthbound flight!

I'd like to share some of my thoughts on life today!

Life today is more speculative than ever with all of the complicated, critical, malicious issues overwhelming America and the world.

It can feel as if we're bridled by an unrewarding state of existence, a normal state of being out of reach.

We long for a conduit, a way that puts life back in touch with the stable, sound, consistent, livable reality we've lost.

The Good news, everything society needs rests in the Hands of God and His Son, Christ Jesus. Put your Trust in Him, and be 'lifted' from the pervading sense of disaffection and abnormality. Find that Peace that comes Only from the Lord's Glorified Light and Holy Spirit!

I'd like to share some of my inspirational thoughts!

In our desperation, Lord put us on the path of your Grace and Mercy. We are lost without You, Lord. Help us to challenge the disabling, adverse forces crippling our lives. Show us the way to Your Light that shines before this darkened wall of life.

Lord, you are at the core of my being, revive my soul, lead me to Hope eternal and Peace that rests in You alone.

An Indefinable Journey

We're on an indefinable, uncertain, adversarial Journey. It almost seems we're being held captive by an onslaught of plaguing, brutal issues subtracting from our fullest experience-for certain possible joy has been put on hold.

Only 'Jesus Christ' can keep us from succumbing to this wretched journey we're on. A path of 'Total Restoration' comes Only through recognizing Him, and His Love for us.

GOD'S HOLY LIGHT

I revel in this wayward time, distant life mingling with rhyme-upon a dim-filled, slumbering day, my mind is seized by this display-following reveries' deep, deep trail, it is not possible to fail.

Familiar, am I with the outskirts of life…plus, I exist

with immense isolation. I have the marvelous experience of being in the palm of the open sky-I like to look into the sanctuary of nature, to that place which survives beyond view. There is in everybody's time, a place lost, and rediscovered, and I enjoy peering into that sacred, hallowed ground.

Simplicity, peace and serenity bound up, persuade and enrich my spirit, aiming me toward a place of permanence

and restfulness. My spirit gets renewed by glimpses and

visions of places and spaces filled with God's Holy Light.

Inside of Silence

A voluminous silence is transferring its difficult reproductions of life.

We're passing through deeply-troubled waters...images and visions of Light and Hope have been weakened.

I Thank You, Lord for the capacity to endure and rise above the destructive waves, avoiding through Your Grace the total disasters for self and soul sinful nature has wrought.

You, Jesus, have brought us safely over crossroads....

Your Spirit lifts us to joy from unexpected dangers and toils,

I could not trust life stretched before the paths I view without Your shield against the fraudulent mystery and magic of living-the nothingness of life without you.

God, inside of silence Your Majestic Grand Will stays in my gaze.

Sharing my Springtime thoughts

The other day, my eyes caught a mother bird gather some twigs and fly off to build a nest. And looking around I saw spring coming alive in the budding trees and greenery, and blooming day lilies. From my backyard I viewed a lofty green heavily-branched evergreen seeming to harbor a deep placid existence. But it was looking into the prevailing sunlight in the surroundings beyond my home this morning that I realized the preponderance of what I'd witnessed this Springtime. It was the presence of the Lord's intrinsic Light, His Holy governance over nature, and overall.

Not the 'America' We 'Thought' We Knew

A calamitous strain has invaded society. We barely recognize life on these shores, it's not the America we thought we knew.

On these shores of America, with everything so adversarial and disruptive going on, faced with such a disfigured society, we're unsettled, out-of-step, lost.

Traveling through these troubled dark waters, reach for the Hand of God for the way. Only His Hand can lift us out of these horrific earthly matters, and restore-put us in touch with an even better life than the America we thought we knew.

My message of Inspiration:

Society has taken life in the wrong direction, and suffering for it. Far too many are ‘care-free’ and ‘self-absorbed’.

Try relying on the Lord, allow Him to Light the way with His ‘Goodness’ and ‘Truth’.

THE CROSS TO THE PRESENT

Because Jesus Christ died on the cross we live with His spirit in us. Through His suffering and dying we are able to confront the ravages of life. He has made our burdens light.

God sent His only Son, Jesus Christ to die a horrible death on our behalf. He had seen enough of the wicked nature of this world, and the suffering of His children on earth. We are in constant battle with a world trying to alienate us from Him and the protection He provides.

From the Cross to the present we have been absolved of all of our wrong doings. Because of Salvation we were given through the tremendous sacrifice of our Lord and Savior Jesus Christ we are safe from world assault and damnation. It is through our Faith in Him that we can overcome the sorrow, grief and misery concentrated all around us.

"'Straighten up, and Fly Right'"

That's my message for today. The idea came to me from the old song I remember from when I was a very young child. At the time, "Straighten Up, and Fly Right" was a popular song associated with grown-ups.

Looking at todays' reckless, degenerate society, that song presents 'Good Advice'.

I don't know about you, but I Thank the Lord that despite such societal unrighteousness and abomination, His Holy Spirit and Graciousness inspires, reinvents, and lifts me to higher, better places and spaces in a crude, disabled world that needs to straighten up and fly right.

I'd like to share some encouraging words:

With the many encumbering, difficult experiences challenging life on earth, know that you can be transformed if you'll allow the Lord to deposit His Devine Spirit of Light into your lives.

THE CHRISTIAN'S JOURNEY

Think about how you've made your way
in this intrinsic, darkly-plated world,
how far you've come from the holocaustic
shores.
Welcome the things gesturing-instances of
goodness and beauty God installed in life. Put
to rest the hurt and assault you've experienced and
stored.
Allow the unifying Holy Spirit to spring up
and with reconnecting, solidifying peace
rescue the desperate Soul.

Today, I'd like share two of my Seasonal poems.

Two Seasonal Poems I'm Sharing

AN APPEALLING SNOWY GRAY BACKGROUND
I relish the call of life in the snowy gray background,
Nature's matter that I view.
A quiet sight echoes, amid chaos I have found.
I experience a good measure of coping tucked in
the distance and all 'round.
I'm transported in the arms of a
peaceful snowy gray background.

A CRITICAL LOOK AT FEBRUARY
A critical look at 'February' means we will get to know…
January's gone, with some of its ice and snow…
Deep, shadowy…and silent as a dorm….
(twist December's solstice and March's equinox), it's
Winter's darkest form…..
Raven-black and somber, it can appear bereft…and have
the haunting presence some middle-earth has left…
A posture on its landscape can open Cupid's door…
Indeed February's no dark stranger any more…
Legacies of pride it has, like Martin Luther King….
February's optimism gets brightened up by Spring.

HELLO EVERYONE

I'd like to let you know that I'm one of the guest authors appearing at the Authors & Speakers Event taking place 7pm Thursday, January 28th. It's a 'zoomed' program.

If you're interested in attending, contact information is in the promotion below.

Thinking Spiritually

Thinking spiritually, God's 'Wondrous' spirit encases everything; He's a reflection interpreting 'purpose' and 'truth' beyond life's 'veiled, maze' experience!

God's Enabling Spirit

Although dismaying, disquieting, and horrendous circumstances confront Americans, and societies around the world, we cannot resign ourselves to those conditions. We must realize that we're Not confined to a position that appears unsolvable, and even pathetic, and combat with God's 'enabling spirit' of resistance and resilience.

He's In Control

Despite the disabling, dismantling, destructive fronts occupying life, making life incomprehensible and difficult to navigate, silence your worries with the knowledge and Truth that the Lord's Promise of Goodness and Mercy lauds, reigns, and He's in 'Control'.

BE ENCOURAGED

WISHING EVERYONE A HAPPY, HEALTHIER NEW YEAR!!!

The year 'Twenty- Twenty' demonstrated just how 'Bad' life could become!

Nevertheless, with all of the horror we experienced since the impact of the Covid-19 Virus, we learned what it feels like to be absolutely 'vulnerable'. The Virus' powerful effect revealed more about us than anything else could—that we're not so solidly in 'Control' as we thought and lived.

The Corona Virus taught us that there is No 'distinction' or 'exception' within the human race according to safety or protection, no one is isolated from life all around us.

Over the period of captivity the 'Wrecking Ball' Virus caused, society was forced to release itself from a sense of self-direction, and compromise and adopt the new inhibiting lifestyle prescribed — what a "Severe Adaptation" that was!!!

Looking at Twenty-Twenty-One, the 'darkened' horizon looks 'Brighter' with the Vaccines becoming Available!

One Snowy Sunday

It was early on a winter Sunday morning. Snow had fallen overnight installing a blanket of white over The Bottom, a working class section of Philadelphia where I grew up. I must have been around nine years old. The four of us, my two sisters and brother and I slumbered to the white-clad, soundless spirit whispering throughout the small row house on the narrow street where we lived.

"Wake up, children. It snowed last night, but we're goin' to Sunday School and church anyway." My mother's southern-tinged, lilting voice awoke me from a soft dream. The aroma of a southern breakfast funneled the quiet, homey atmosphere. "Your father can't move the car, so we will have ta walk to church."

In my excitement about the snow, I jumped down from the top bunk where I slept, and in break-neck speed was at the window marveling the snowfall. My brother, Roddy, and two sisters, Joan and Margaret also broke from their beds and quickly took places at the window. Below, what appeared to be a foot of snow, untouched and smooth as meringue, lathered our narrow street.

Following a breakfast of biscuits, cheese and eggs, bacon, grits, my family dressed and began walking the six blocks to church. The mammoth snowfall had closed all of the businesses and stores. Snow had cast a magical, nostalgic spell over the still surroundings. The magic deepened over a shoe repair shop and other shops and stores. (The wood frame, worn-looking shoe shop seemed to revel in the simple, pleasant past it revived. An aged Woolworth Five and Dime still in its original red brick building naturally and appealingly restored an olden time of red fire engines and carrousels. And other stores and businesses as well appeared to be cloaked in nostalgia from an old-fashioned spirit).

Some tracks had just been cleared and a trolley was chugging down Lancaster Avenue as my family continued trudging toward church.

A WANDERING LIGHT

There's something there, translated in the wilderness of life… a wandering light, shallow in a space of time, escaped from a place of permanence-a roving minstrel singing rhyme, wispy and elusive in the mind, a current of universal goodness just around the bend, the Creators' wandering light, inspiration for all mankind.

VETERANS DAY

I'd like to express my Thanks to all who've served and sacrificed for the freedoms we can experience in America!!!

I'd like to add that in our immediate family— Huey, our son Vernon and I are Proud all three of us to have served in the United States Air Force. Huey and Vernon gave lengthy Service-retiring after more than twenty years, while I served a very short period, but served nonetheless.

God Bless America!

From a small beginning I was bound for higher ground. Against multiple disquieting passages and places, I thank God for that richer, spiritual place I have found, areas in life for which I strived.

I Thank the Lord for the 'Gifts' He has given me that have allowed me to live Inspired!

www.ingramcontent.com/pod-product-compliance
Lightning Source LLC
Chambersburg PA
CBHW050018170726
48282CB00025B/453
9788119228805